Little RIDDLERS

Surrey

Edited By Julie Macdonald

First published in Great Britain in 2018 by:

Young Writers
Remus House
Coltsfoot Drive
Peterborough
PE2 9BF
Telephone: 01733 890066
Website: www.youngwriters.co.uk

All Rights Reserved
Book Design by Ashley Janson
© Copyright Contributors 2018
SB ISBN 978-1-78896-436-4
Printed and bound in the UK by BookPrintingUK
Website: www.bookprintinguk.com
YB0359P

FOREWORD

Dear Reader,

Are you ready to get your thinking caps on to puzzle your way through this wonderful collection?

Young Writers' Little Riddlers competition set out to encourage young writers to create their own riddles. Their answers could be whatever or whoever their imaginations desired; from people to places, animals to objects, food to seasons. Riddles are a great way to further the children's use of poetic expression, including onomatopoeia and similes, as well as encourage them to 'think outside the box' by providing clues without giving the answer away immediately.

All of us here at Young Writers believe in the importance of inspiring young children to produce creative writing, including poetry, and we feel that seeing their own riddles in print will keep that creative spirit burning brightly and proudly.

We hope you enjoy riddling your way through this book as much as we enjoyed reading all the entries.

CONTENTS

Bell Farm Primary School, Hersham

Annabelle Tay (6)	1
Toby Starkey (5)	2
Gabriel Sorbello (6)	3
Oscar Conway (7)	4
Chloe Parling (5)	5
Ryley John Paul Alexander-Howe (6)	6
Emily-Rose Holtom (7)	7
Gordon Woolger (7)	8
Lani Bradley (7)	9
Emma Brooker (7)	10
Chloe Blum (5)	11
Holly Rebecca Burns (6)	12

Holy Trinity CE Primary & Nursery School, Richmond

Nina Nakyejwe-Kintu (7)	13
Mary Frith (7)	14
Aramis Kareem Murray (6)	15
Seah Han (6)	16
Ella Rose Klee (7)	17
Kitty Streek (7)	18
Maisie Annaly (7)	19
Saim Karim (6)	20
Danielle Oye-Somefun (6)	21
Vilian Rodrigues (7)	22
Frankie Meikle (7)	23
Lina Arrigo (7)	24
Lois Haughan (6)	25
Caitlin Joy Lorenzo (6)	26
Max Ottenhof (6)	27
Jacob Seed (7)	28
Leo Chesters (6)	29
Brielle Grace Lorenzo (6)	30

Perseid School, Morden

Riylee Shearwood (6)	31
Daniel Baah Yeboah (6)	32

St Cyprian's Greek Orthodox Primary Academy, Thornton Heath

Micah James Adalgo Richards (7)	33
Jessica Alves Da Silva (5)	34
Miranda Sophia Tsoukkas (7)	35
Joanna Walker (6)	36
Sebastian Carr (7)	37
Nicholas	38
Thomas Buckle (6)	39
Stelios Tsoukkas (5)	40
Aaria Sardar (7)	41
Juliet Asianaa (7)	42
Eilish Richards (6)	43
Uchechukwu Francis Chidera Okoji (6)	44
Joel Asiedu-Yeboah (7)	45
Manna Michael (6)	46
Nhyira Addotey (6)	47
Micah Spencer-Campbell (6)	48
Athina Kapelas (7)	49
Ebun Alabi (6)	50
Neriah Wesley (6)	51
Adriana Esmie Muriel Prescod (7)	52
Betania Solomon (6)	53

Ivor Franklin Stack (6)	54
Victoria-Vasiliki Saloum (6)	55
Cheryl Adu-Gyamfi (7)	56
Michael Martins (7)	57
Papa Osei-Bonsu (7)	58
Jaleel Meerun (6)	59
Nathan Adabie-Ankarh (7)	60
Daniel Adegbite (7)	61
Gabriella Tallis-Flynn (5)	62
Kwaku Poku Afreh (6)	63
Isaiah Allen (6)	64
Faith-Ann Roseman (7)	65
Jacob Bradbury (5)	66
Aiyanna Holder (6)	67
Kenzo Harris (5)	68
Ioanna Angeliki Fa (7)	69
Dana Colina De Sousa (6)	70
Isaiah Amponsah (5)	71
Daniel Lewita (7)	72
Dara Ajibola (6)	73
Jack Nevens (6)	74
Marlea McCleary-Collins (6)	75
Nicole Kakembo (5)	76
Omari Walters (6)	77
Amber Miller-Houston (5)	78
Jenny Ma (6)	79
Remel Hutchinson (6)	80
Mia Freitas Nobrega (5)	81
Tseyone Kalekidan (6)	82
Michelle Darko (7)	83
Isabelly Mendonca-Alves (5)	84
Anna-Maria Cherri (5)	85
Ramarn White (5)	86
George Stylinanou (6)	87

St Peter's CE Primary School, Wrecclesham

Bethany Lee (7)	88
Megan Marriage (7)	89
Jake Collins (7)	90
Harry Preston (7)	91
Lyla Mae Davies (6)	92
Samuel Pressly (7)	93

Evie Burr (6)	94
Sadie Arthur (6)	95
Rhema Jeboda (6)	96
Dexter Philcox (7)	97
Matilda Ambrose (7)	98
Evelyn Ann Pearson (7)	99
George Thomas Bryan (6)	100
Lena Michaelides (6)	101
Isla Mae Tudor (7)	102
Lexie Puttick (7)	103
Holly Harris (6)	104
Jessica Carys Ann Black (6)	105
Haydn Woodhouse (7)	106
Lucas Pinto (7)	107
Emilia Grace Collinson (6)	108
Poppy Chua (7)	109
Sophie Farrant (6)	110
Kara Burch (6)	111
Amelie Kelley (6)	112
Zane Harman (6)	113
Sharae Rattigan (6)	114
Rylan Tucker (6)	115
Victor Finn (7)	116
Chloe Scother (6)	117
Labeena Tahir (6)	118
Jamie Potter (6)	119
Patrick Doherty (6)	120
Dex Woods (7)	121

The Dawnay School, Great Brookham

Matilda Harris (6)	122
Paloma Rose Pardo (5)	123
Elly Edling-Hill (5)	124
Sophie McIntosh (6)	125
Eleanor Rourke (5)	126
Joseph Osmond Gorman (5)	127
Thomas Jenner (6)	128
Ruby Lane (5)	129
Riley Williams (6)	130
Francesca Louise Vlaeminck-Thomas (6)	131
Lilly Ozturk (6)	132

Gloria Altersberger (5)	133
Luca Favero (6)	134
Georgina Hallett (5)	135
Fred John Pilling (5)	136
Zac Lawrence (5)	137
Freddie Stephens (5)	138

The Russell School, Richmond

Evelyn Archer (7)	139
Josephine Elizabeth Bryant (6)	140
Sienna Scruby (6)	141
Aurelia Kate Powell-Blyth (6)	142
Robert Raguzin (7)	143
Henry Grimm (7)	144
Tasneem Sumaya Djerfi (7)	145
Sara Straffi (7)	146

Wood Street Infant School, Guildford

Amelia Fear (6)	147
Jakub Miucci (5)	148

THE POEMS

Furry Cutie

I am a mammal.
I live in a very cold place.
I have thick fur to keep myself warm.
I have a bushy tail.
I change the colour of my fur with the seasons.
I am not fussy with my food.
I eat whatever I can find.
What am I?

Answer: An Arctic fox.

Annabelle Tay (6)
Bell Farm Primary School, Hersham

Build Me Up

I can come in many different shapes and sizes.
I can be any colour of the rainbow.
I am made out of plastic.
You can put me together.
My studs make me famous.
You can make anything with me.
What am I?

Answer: Lego.

Toby Starkey (5)
Bell Farm Primary School, Hersham

The Happy Swimmer

I live underwater and I'm covered in scales.
I don't have lungs.
I breathe through my gills.
I can be a pet.
I don't have smelly feet!
There are over 32,000 of us.
What am I?

Answer: A fish.

Gabriel Sorbello (6)
Bell Farm Primary School, Hersham

Lightning Fury!

I am small and yellow.
I am very powerful.
My master's name is Ash.
I always help my friends.
I look like a type of rabbit.
I am a Pokémon figure.
What am I?

Answer: I am Pikachu.

Oscar Conway (7)
Bell Farm Primary School, Hersham

The Tree

I live in Africa.
Lions like to try to eat me.
I have lots of spots.
I eat lots of leaves.
My tongue is long.
I can reach up high.
I have a long neck.
What am I?

Answer: A giraffe.

Chloe Parling (5)
Bell Farm Primary School, Hersham

What Am I?

I am big.
I make a roaring sound.
I am furry.
I eat meat.
I eat other animals.
I sleep in a den.
I am coming to get you.
Roar, roar, roar.
What am I?

Answer: A lion.

Ryley John Paul Alexander-Howe (6)
Bell Farm Primary School, Hersham

Shiny

I turn off and on.
I flicker and shine.
I can be dim or bright.
I stay in the room by myself.
I create shadows.
I also come from the sun.
What am I?

Answer: Light.

Emily-Rose Holtom (7)
Bell Farm Primary School, Hersham

Cold

I'm very cold.
Sometimes I snow.
You will find animals hibernating.
You can see me everywhere.
The days are short.
I don't eat.
What am I?

Answer: Winter.

Gordon Woolger (7)
Bell Farm Primary School, Hersham

Furry Friends

I have a round fluffy tail.
I can be a pet.
I have four legs.
I eat carrots.
I have a fluffy dark grey body.
I have long ears.
What am I?

Answer: A rabbit

Lani Bradley (7)
Bell Farm Primary School, Hersham

Writing Writing

I am long and skinny.
I am made of wood.
I am a cylinder.
I have a pointy end.
I have lead inside me.
You can write with me.
What am I?

Answer: A pencil.

Emma Brooker (7)
Bell Farm Primary School, Hersham

Berrylicious

It's juicy.
It's red and green.
I like to eat it.
You can pick your own.
It's like a heart.
I love it.
What am I?

Answer: A strawberry.

Chloe Blum (5)
Bell Farm Primary School, Hersham

Purr

I scratch and I purr.
I am soft to stroke.
I can be black.
I eat mice.
I have whiskers.
What am I?

Answer: A cat.

Holly Rebecca Burns (6)
Bell Farm Primary School, Hersham

I Am The Queen

I wear a crown.
You never see me frown.
I rule a country.
I live in a palace.
I am rich, I am old.
I'm in the royal family.
I am a great grandmother.
I have been on the throne for sixty-five years.
I am the longest reining monarch.
I am protected by guards and have a royal army.
I live in a big palace in central London.
I have grey curly hair.
Who am I?

Answer: Queen Elizabeth II.

Nina Nakyejwe-Kintu (7)
Holy Trinity CE Primary & Nursery School, Richmond

Cuddles

I am fluffy and grey.
I live high up in the trees.
This is where I find my food.
I am a marsupial and I am as soft as a teddy bear.
I'm only found in the southern hemisphere.
My mummy keeps me safe on her back.
I'm a very sleepy animal.
What am I?

Answer: A koala.

Mary Frith (7)
Holy Trinity CE Primary & Nursery School, Richmond

Deep In The Snow

I live in the snowiest, darkest caves.
I'm white with black spots.
I am quite small.
I am the best at hiding in the snow.
I love eating mountain goats.
I am very swift.
I look like snow, so much you wouldn't see me!
What am I?

Answer: A snow leopard.

Aramis Kareem Murray (6)
Holy Trinity CE Primary & Nursery School, Richmond

Slow Power

I have a hard shell.
I have dirty nails.
I lay eggs in the sand.
I live in water or on land.
I like cucumber.
I move slowly.
I don't need an umbrella.
I don't worry about the rain.
I swim fast in the water.
What am I?

Answer: A turtle.

Seah Han (6)
Holy Trinity CE Primary & Nursery School, Richmond

Magic

I use my magic to control the wood.
I am the queen of the woods.
I have glimmering blue eyes.
I have curly hair.
I have a horn on my head.
I always wear a pretty bow in my hair.
I have a fluffy pink nose.
What am I?

Answer: A unicorn.

Ella Rose Klee (7)
Holy Trinity CE Primary & Nursery School, Richmond

I've Got To Clip Clop

I can take you for a ride if you want.
I can run fast and jump.
I wear shoes while I sleep.
I like to have sugar cubes as a treat.
You can plait my hair if you like.
But don't mix me up with a bike.
What am I?

Answer: A horse.

Kitty Streek (7)
Holy Trinity CE Primary & Nursery School, Richmond

Sweet Jackets

I have an eye, but I can't see.
I come in different shapes and sizes.
I can be yellow, red, orange and white.
I contain a lot of vitamin C.
I grow in the ground.
I can be new, I can be sweet.
What am I?

Answer: A potato.

Maisie Annaly (7)
Holy Trinity CE Primary & Nursery School, Richmond

Wash, Wash, Wash

You can turn me both ways, left or right.
I can come in many different colours.
I can be cold or hot.
Sometimes I am full or not.
My tears can burn you.
I can be long or I can be short.
What am I?

Answer: A tap.

Saim Karim (6)
Holy Trinity CE Primary & Nursery School, Richmond

My Friend

I have brown fur.
I have a great sense of smell.
I come in different shapes and sizes.
I protect my family.
I can hunt and I can be very helpful.
I am a girl's best friend.
What am I?

Answer: A dog.

Danielle Oye-Somefun (6)
Holy Trinity CE Primary & Nursery School, Richmond

Tick-Tock

Bright and big.
Tock-tick
To wake me up.
Gulp, gulp.
It's time to walk.
Time to play,
And in bed to lay.
Can you guess what this riddle says?

Answer: *Tick-tock I am a clock.*

Vilian Rodrigues (7)
Holy Trinity CE Primary & Nursery School, Richmond

Gigantic

I am a giant creature.
I cannot jump at all.
I have a very long nose.
I don't forget anything!
I love swimming in the cool water.
My family are very special to me.
What am I?

Answer: An elephant.

Frankie Meikle (7)
Holy Trinity CE Primary & Nursery School, Richmond

A Swirly Surprise

I am very sticky.
I am a type of candy.
I sit on a stick.
If you eat too many of me, you'll be sick.
I don't think dentists like me.
But I make children happy.
What am I?

Answer: A lollipop.

Lina Arrigo (7)
Holy Trinity CE Primary & Nursery School, Richmond

Right Royal Riddle

I am fluffy with a wet, black nose.
I am small and cute.
My ears are pointy.
My name means dwarf dog.
The Queen loves me, she has five of me.
What am I?

Answer: A corgi!

Lois Haughan (6)
Holy Trinity CE Primary & Nursery School, Richmond

Meek And Great

You ride on me.
I have long ears.
I live in a stable.
I am grey.
I have small black eyes.
I make a sound.
What am I?

Answer: A donkey.

Caitlin Joy Lorenzo (6)
Holy Trinity CE Primary & Nursery School, Richmond

The Helper

I help people with learning.
I add, subtract, divide and times.
I like arrays.
I like to group and use number lines.
What am I?

Answer: Maths.

Max Ottenhof (6)
Holy Trinity CE Primary & Nursery School, Richmond

I Own The Ocean

I live in the ocean.
I'm big and grey.
My teeth are sharp.
My tail does smell.
I love to be scary.
What am I?

Answer: A shark.

Jacob Seed (7)
Holy Trinity CE Primary & Nursery School, Richmond

I'm A Cut Above The Rest

I am a cut above the rest.
What I do, I'm the best.
I can cut so use me safe.
Use me responsibly.
What am I?

Answer: Scissors.

Leo Chesters (6)
Holy Trinity CE Primary & Nursery School, Richmond

Black And White

I'm black and white.
I'm big.
But hunters look for me.
I climb trees.
What am I?

Answer: A panda.

Brielle Grace Lorenzo (6)
Holy Trinity CE Primary & Nursery School, Richmond

Splashes

I feel waves.
I smell sand.
I hear a shark.
I taste bubbles.
I see green.
Where am I?

Answer: Under the sea.

Riylee Shearwood (6)
Perseid School, Morden

Deep Blue

I smell starfish.
I see bubbles.
I hear noises.
I feel air.
Where am I?

Answer: Underwater.

Daniel Baah Yeboah (6)
Perseid School, Morden

Super Spikes

I had spikes on my back
I had a long tail.
I had a long neck.
I had four legs.
I used to eat leaves.
I used to get eaten by a T-rex.
I drank water from the river.
My legs were 25cms long.
I used to run quite fast.
I had sharp teeth.
What was I?

Answer: A stegosaurus.

Micah James Adalgo Richards (7)
St Cyprian's Greek Orthodox Primary Academy, Thornton Heath

Pedal Power

I come in different styles.
You can ride on me for miles.
When I appear, *ting-ting* you may hear.
I have a very comfy seat.
I have two pedals, but no stinky feet.
I have a chain.
Riding uphill on me can cause pain.
What am I?

Answer: A bicycle.

Jessica Alves Da Silva (5)
St Cyprian's Greek Orthodox Primary Academy, Thornton Heath

Mythical Horse

I have a spiraling horn and beautiful Pegasus wings.
If you pass me by, I will run and fly.
I have magical powers that help me get to the sky.
Try and try but you won't succeed.
There is no way of catching me.
What am I?

Answer: A unicorn.

Miranda Sophia Tsoukkas (7)
St Cyprian's Greek Orthodox Primary Academy, Thornton Heath

Claws

I am not naughty.
I have claws and jaws.
I do have stinky feet.
I have strong legs.
I have a smelly tail.
I am not the strongest.
I am the cutest dinosaur.
I am nice.
I am not frightening.
What am I?

Answer: A triceratops.

Joanna Walker (6)
St Cyprian's Greek Orthodox Primary Academy, Thornton Heath

Spot Round

I am very round and big.
I have black spots.
I have more white than black.
You can play with me on the grass.
I am played with in big places.
I have writing on me.
I live in a changing room.
What am I?

Answer: A football.

Sebastian Carr (7)
St Cyprian's Greek Orthodox Primary Academy, Thornton Heath

What Am I?

You need an apron for this job.
It is a very messy job.
All the stuff dries up on you.
And the stuff is colourful.
It can be oil based and come in water colours too.
All this stuff is paint.
What am I?

Answer: An artist.

Nicholas
St Cyprian's Greek Orthodox Primary Academy, Thornton Heath

What Am I?

I am so frosty and cold.
I only come out in winter days.
Lots of people make me what I am.
I wear a hat and a scarf.
I have a carrot for my nose.
And I have sticks for my arms.
What am I?

Answer: A snowman.

Thomas Buckle (6)
St Cyprian's Greek Orthodox Primary Academy, Thornton Heath

In The Winter

I live in the snow.
I blow the snow.
If sunshine comes I will melt into the grass.
I have three buttons.
I am white with stick arms and a carrot nose.
I can't move at all.
What am I?

Answer: A snowman.

Stelios Tsoukkas (5)
St Cyprian's Greek Orthodox Primary Academy, Thornton Heath

Fly High

Fly high, fly high.
Hold on tight as it flies away.
It can get caught in the wind.
It can fly away and get lost.
Sometimes it can loop the loop.
It can fly like a balloon.
What is it?

Answer: A kite.

Aaria Sardar (7)
St Cyprian's Greek Orthodox Primary Academy, Thornton Heath

Fairy

I have magic powers.
I have my magical magic wand.
I have a special crown.
I have a pretty dress.
I take something and leave you with a coin.
I'm very tiny.
What am I?

Answer: The tooth fairy.

Juliet Asianaa (7)
St Cyprian's Greek Orthodox Primary Academy, Thornton Heath

What Is It?

It is super hairy.
It can come in any colour.
We use it in numeracy when we are counting.
You can build with it.
It has a hole.
It has a sticking thing.
What is it?

Answer: A numeracy cube.

Eilish Richards (6)
St Cyprian's Greek Orthodox Primary Academy, Thornton Heath

Yummy

I am round.
You love me just like most people.
I can be cut into slices, so many can eat me.
I am baked with crust.
And I am much better with cheese and pepperoni.
What am I?

Answer: A pizza.

Uchechukwu Francis Chidera Okoji (6)
St Cyprian's Greek Orthodox Primary Academy, Thornton Heath

Up And Down And Away!

I have two number level buttons.
I can go up and down.
I can say where are you going.
I open and close myself.
I have an alarm button.
I have a fan lock.
What am I?

Answer: A lift.

Joel Asiedu-Yeboah (7)
St Cyprian's Greek Orthodox Primary Academy, Thornton Heath

Fluttery Soft Creature

Everyone looks at me because I'm so beautiful.
I am colourful.
I have lots of patterns.
I can fly.
I can't swim.
I am first a caterpillar.
What am I?

Answer: A butterfly.

Manna Michael (6)
St Cyprian's Greek Orthodox Primary Academy, Thornton Heath

What Is It?

It is always on wheels.
But it doesn't fall.
It is always working.
You use a lot of energy.
Riding up mountains is painful.
Riding is the best.
What is it?

Answer: A bicycle.

Nhyira Addotey (6)
St Cyprian's Greek Orthodox Primary Academy, Thornton Heath

What Am I?

I make a loud noise.
I don't eat.
I have to drive lots of times.
I have a window on the front of me.
I have an engine.
I have two wheels.
What am I?

Answer: A motorbike.

Micah Spencer-Campbell (6)
St Cyprian's Greek Orthodox Primary Academy, Thornton Heath

What Am I?

I am a princess
But you don't know my name.
I am looking for a mirror to help me.
There is someone who will die in my family.
I am a Disney princess.
Who am I?

Answer: Moana.

Athina Kapelas (7)
St Cyprian's Greek Orthodox Primary Academy, Thornton Heath

A Fruit

It is yellow and sometimes green.
Does not have juice, it is dry, yummy.
It is a fruit, people eat it.
It has skin on it.
Inside it is yummy.
What is it?

Answer: A banana.

Ebun Alabi (6)
St Cyprian's Greek Orthodox Primary Academy, Thornton Heath

What Am I?

I have a big neck.
I have four legs.
I eat an apple.
I have a long neck.
I have some dots on my body.
I have a tail on my bottom.
What am I?

Answer: A giraffe.

Neriah Wesley (6)
St Cyprian's Greek Orthodox Primary Academy, Thornton Heath

The Cat Family

I am furry and cute.
My favourite food is cat food.
My fear is dogs.
I don't like other cats.
If they come near me I will fight them.
What am I?

Answer: A cat.

Adriana Esmie Muriel Prescod (7)
St Cyprian's Greek Orthodox Primary Academy, Thornton Heath

What Am I?

I am very furry.
I am also very soft.
I am also tall.
I am very loud.
I am the strongest in the world.
But I am loved by children.
What am I?

Answer: A lion.

Betania Solomon (6)
St Cyprian's Greek Orthodox Primary Academy, Thornton Heath

What Am I?

I have scales.
I'm dangerous to touch.
I am long.
I hide a lot.
I am so fierce.
I lived with the dinosaurs.
What am I?

Answer: A crocodile.

Ivor Franklin Stack (6)
St Cyprian's Greek Orthodox Primary Academy, Thornton Heath

What Am I?

I live in the lake and I swim.
I swim all day and I see people.
I look at people when they pass by.
I look and swim and swim.
What am I?

Answer: A swan.

Victoria-Vasiliki Saloum (6)
St Cyprian's Greek Orthodox Primary Academy, Thornton Heath

The Small Creature

I have a furry body.
I do not roar loudly.
I have very sharp claws.
I am very cute and beautiful.
Some people love me.
What am I?

Answer: A cat.

Cheryl Adu-Gyamfi (7)
St Cyprian's Greek Orthodox Primary Academy, Thornton Heath

Hairy I Am

I am so hairy.
I make a funny noise.
I live up in trees.
I am very crazy.
I scratch myself.
I love bananas.
What am I?

Answer: A monkey.

Michael Martins (7)
St Cyprian's Greek Orthodox Primary Academy, Thornton Heath

What Am I?

I have got sharp teeth.
I am fast.
I eat other animals.
I am the best.
I am scary like a lion.
I do fight.
What am I?

Answer: A tiger.

Papa Osei-Bonsu (7)
St Cyprian's Greek Orthodox Primary Academy, Thornton Heath

What Am I?

I am small.
I have stretchy hands.
I can grow as big as a snake.
I can climb in the trees.
I can run fast.
What am I?

Answer: A lizard.

Jaleel Meerun (6)
St Cyprian's Greek Orthodox Primary Academy, Thornton Heath

Pride

I am so fierce.
I am king of the jungle.
I have four legs.
I have a very nice mane.
I also have a long tail.
What am I?

Answer: A lion.

Nathan Adabie-Ankarh (7)
St Cyprian's Greek Orthodox Primary Academy, Thornton Heath

I Slither

My body is long and round.
In the jungle I am found.
When I move, I make no sound.
I slither across the ground.
What am I?

Answer: A snake.

Daniel Adegbite (7)
St Cyprian's Greek Orthodox Primary Academy, Thornton Heath

What Am I?

I have lots of colours.
I have sugar in me.
I give you brain freeze.
I am ice.
There is lots of me.
What am I?

Answer: An ice cream.

Gabriella Tallis-Flynn (5)
St Cyprian's Greek Orthodox Primary Academy, Thornton Heath

What Am I?

I am the best at kicking a ball.
I am good at scoring goals.
I am a football fan.
I am good at coaching.
What am I?

Answer: A footballer.

Kwaku Poku Afreh (6)
St Cyprian's Greek Orthodox Primary Academy, Thornton Heath

What Am I?

I can sting people.
I can scare people.
I make honey.
I sleep in the high trees.
I can go in the house.
What am I?

Answer: A bee.

Isaiah Allen (6)
St Cyprian's Greek Orthodox Primary Academy, Thornton Heath

Zippery

I am made out of snow.
I have a carrot nose.
My nose is orange.
I am sometimes made at Christmas time.
What am I?

Answer: A snowman.

Faith-Ann Roseman (7)
St Cyprian's Greek Orthodox Primary Academy, Thornton Heath

Who Am I?

I am married to Prince Charles.
I am loved by people.
I wear high heeled shoes.
I can invite you to tea.
Who am I?

Answer: Camilla.

Jacob Bradbury (5)
St Cyprian's Greek Orthodox Primary Academy, Thornton Heath

Princess Diana

I am very nice.
I am royal.
I am friendly.
I am special.
I am famous.
I am wonderful
What am I?

Answer: A princess.

Aiyanna Holder (6)
St Cyprian's Greek Orthodox Primary Academy, Thornton Heath

Explode Lava

It sometimes erupts.
The rocks are called magma.
It lives in the ocean.
It has burning lava.
What is it?

Answer: A volcano.

Kenzo Harris (5)
St Cyprian's Greek Orthodox Primary Academy, Thornton Heath

I Love Animals

I have two long ears.
I can jump.
My tail is round.
I can be a pet.
And I love carrots.
What am I?

Answer: A rabbit.

Ioanna Angeliki Fa (7)
St Cyprian's Greek Orthodox Primary Academy, Thornton Heath

What Am I?

I am grey.
I am big.
My tummy is big and fat.
I have a big trunk.
I have big legs.
What am I?

Answer: An elephant.

Dana Colina De Sousa (6)
St Cyprian's Greek Orthodox Primary Academy, Thornton Heath

What Am I?

I eat meat.
I eat people.
I have a tail.
I am the king of the jungle.
I am fierce.
What am I?

Answer: A lion.

Isaiah Amponsah (5)
St Cyprian's Greek Orthodox Primary Academy, Thornton Heath

What Am I?

I love to eat fish.
I don't have ears.
I don't eat mammals.
I cannot swim.
What am I?

Answer: A pterodactyl.

Daniel Lewita (7)
St Cyprian's Greek Orthodox Primary Academy, Thornton Heath

Who Am I?

I am very long.
I have a black tongue.
I have a big mouth.
I have a pattern.
What am I?

Answer: An anaconda.

Dara Ajibola (6)
St Cyprian's Greek Orthodox Primary Academy, Thornton Heath

What Am I?

I have a bed.
I have a long tail.
I can bark.
I have fleas.
I have a lead.
What am I?

Answer: A dog.

Jack Nevens (6)
St Cyprian's Greek Orthodox Primary Academy, Thornton Heath

What Am I?

I am rainbow colours.
I have a heart.
I have yellow hooves.
I have a horn.
What am I?

Answer: A unicorn.

Marlea McCleary-Collins (6)
St Cyprian's Greek Orthodox Primary Academy, Thornton Heath

What Am I?

I am a fruit.
I am loose.
I am healthy for you.
I am wet.
I am sweet.
What am I?

Answer: A grape.

Nicole Kakembo (5)
St Cyprian's Greek Orthodox Primary Academy, Thornton Heath

What Am I?

You can catch me
But you cannot throw?
I make you sneeze.
I make you cough.
What am I?

Answer: A cold.

Omari Walters (6)
St Cyprian's Greek Orthodox Primary Academy, Thornton Heath

What Am I?

I help people when they are poorly.
I wear a white coat.
I make people better.
What am I?

Answer: A doctor.

Amber Miller-Houston (5)
St Cyprian's Greek Orthodox Primary Academy, Thornton Heath

Furry Pet

I have little ears.
I have a long tail.
I like a cuddle.
I'm very soft.
What am I?

Answer: A cat.

Jenny Ma (6)
St Cyprian's Greek Orthodox Primary Academy, Thornton Heath

A Person

I help people.
I wear a white coat.
I tell people to rest for three weeks.
What am I?

Answer: A doctor.

Remel Hutchinson (6)
St Cyprian's Greek Orthodox Primary Academy, Thornton Heath

What Am I?

I have long hair.
I have a long dress.
I have a sister that looks like me.
What am I?

Answer: A twin.

Mia Freitas Nobrega (5)
St Cyprian's Greek Orthodox Primary Academy, Thornton Heath

What Am I?

I have two wheels.
I have pedals.
I have a seat.
I have a bell.
What am I?

Answer: A bicycle.

Tseyone Kalekidan (6)
St Cyprian's Greek Orthodox Primary Academy, Thornton Heath

What Am I?

I have four legs.
I have fur.
If you stroke me, I am going to purr.
What am I?

Answer: A cat.

Michelle Darko (7)
St Cyprian's Greek Orthodox Primary Academy, Thornton Heath

What Am I?

I am kind.
I help people.
I am not rude.
I do injections.
What am I?

Answer: A nurse.

Isabelly Mendonca-Alves (5)
St Cyprian's Greek Orthodox Primary Academy, Thornton Heath

An Object

I have two wheels.
I have one seat.
I have two pedals.
What am I?

Answer: A bicycle.

Anna-Maria Cherri (5)
St Cyprian's Greek Orthodox Primary Academy, Thornton Heath

What Am I?

I have fluffy hair.
I can gobble people up.
I can roar.
What am I?

Answer: A lion.

Ramarn White (5)
St Cyprian's Greek Orthodox Primary Academy, Thornton Heath

What Am I?

My body is soft.
My claws are sharp.
I might bite you.
What am I?

Answer: A lion.

George Stylinanou (6)
St Cyprian's Greek Orthodox Primary Academy, Thornton Heath

What Am I?

I have a very long tail that whacks very hard.
If you come near me I will eat you and kill you.
If you frighten me, I will frighten you back.
I have very long skin that is scaly.
I am very big that my tail will trip you up.
I can be very scary if you come too close to me.
You will get a fright.
What am I?

Answer: A boa constrictor.

Bethany Lee (7)
St Peter's CE Primary School, Wrecclesham

The Boiling Hot Master

I am made of rock.
I spit burning hot things, but I don't have a mouth.
It's very rare for me to explode.
I'm as tall as the biggest mountain.
I can cause you great danger if you wake me from my sleep.
You can climb me if you like, but I'm very steep.
What am I?

Answer: A volcano.

Megan Marriage (7)
St Peter's CE Primary School, Wrecclesham

In The Air

I fly like a dragon.
I am as blue as a blueberry.
I watch out for my prey.
My wings are as flat as a piece of paper.
My body is as thin as hair.
I normally hang out in the air with my friends and family.
What am I?

Answer: A dragonfly.

Jake Collins (7)
St Peter's CE Primary School, Wrecclesham

Whoosh!

My claws are as sharp as a knife.
My eyes are as golden as the sun.
I'm as fierce as a lion.
My coat is the colour of hay.
My spots are the colour of midnight.
I'm the fastest animal in Africa.
What am I?

Answer: A cheetah.

Harry Preston (7)
St Peter's CE Primary School, Wrecclesham

What Am I?

I have a scaly tail.
I stick on trees.
I have a long tongue that sticks out of my mouth.
I have glowing eyes.
I have four green legs.
I slither everywhere in the jungle.
I like to eat flies.
What am I?

Answer: A lizard.

Lyla Mae Davies (6)
St Peter's CE Primary School, Wrecclesham

The Big Sticky Slime

I am very large and I have colossal eyes.
My eyes glow in the dark.
I've got big feet.
I've got massive hands and wide legs.
I've got sharp toes and teeth.
I am hairy and I am green.
What am I?

Answer: A monster.

Samuel Pressly (7)
St Peter's CE Primary School, Wrecclesham

The Hip Hopper

I live underground like a mole.
I have a fluffy body like a tiger.
I have long ears like a donkey.
My white tail is like snow.
I have lots of brothers and sisters.
I can hop as high as a bush.
What am I?

Answer: A bunny.

Evie Burr (6)
St Peter's CE Primary School, Wrecclesham

My Pretty Prancer

I eat leaves and hay.
I have a mane.
It is like coral.
I have hooves that come in any colour.
I have a white smooth body.
You can ride on me like a horse.
I have a multicoloured horn.
What am I?

Answer: A unicorn.

Sadie Arthur (6)
St Peter's CE Primary School, Wrecclesham

Mr Medium

I have biscuits, but I don't eat meat.
You can put a lead on me, but I will run.
I love being stroked.
I am very gentle.
I like to sleep in my warm and cosy bed.
I am fluffy like a bird.
What am I?

Answer: A dog.

Rhema Jeboda (6)
St Peter's CE Primary School, Wrecclesham

Magic Dust

I am made of liquid.
I explode when someone says explode.
I am blue and bubbly.
There are lots of different kinds of me.
I am a magical thing.
Harry Potter uses me to cast spells.
What am I?

Answer: A potion.

Dexter Philcox (7)
St Peter's CE Primary School, Wrecclesham

Smoky Woky

I am as gold as can be.
I shine in the moonlight.
I have a point at the front.
I have a lid too.
When you open the lid there is smoke.
I have someone hiding in inside me.
What am I?

Answer: A genie lamp.

Matilda Ambrose (7)
St Peter's CE Primary School, Wrecclesham

What Am I?

I fly at night.
I glow in the dark and I zoom so fast.
I am smaller than a mouse.
You can't touch me.
You have to go to sleep before I come.
I tiptoe in the dark.
Who am I?

Answer: *The tooth fairy.*

Evelyn Ann Pearson (7)
St Peter's CE Primary School, Wrecclesham

What Am I?

I can climb trees.
I am brown sometimes.
I am weird when I change my colour.
I am sometimes curly.
I don't talk.
I like climbing trees.
I am sometimes funny.
What am I?

Answer: A chameleon.

George Thomas Bryan (6)
St Peter's CE Primary School, Wrecclesham

High Hopper

I have long, pointy ears.
I'm as orange as the desert.
I live in hot, sunny countries.
I jump higher than a frog.
I have a small pouch.
My baby lives in my pouch.
What am I?

Answer: A kangaroo.

Lena Michaelides (6)
St Peter's CE Primary School, Wrecclesham

What Am I?

I live in caves.
I am as black as a scary night.
I have teeth as sharp as knives.
On my skin I have spots.
I like crunching on bones.
My favourite thing to eat is meat.
What am I?

Answer: A hyena.

Isla Mae Tudor (7)
St Peter's CE Primary School, Wrecclesham

What Am I?

I have a furry tail.
I am as fluffy as a panda.
My eyes glow in the dark.
I go outside at night.
I climb into trees and sit in them.
When I jump I always land on my feet.
What am I?

Answer: A cat.

Lexie Puttick (7)
St Peter's CE Primary School, Wrecclesham

Furry Mare

I have a long, fluffy mane.
I can run really fast.
I can jump over obstacles and I can walk.
I have four hooves on my feet.
I am dark brown and beige.
I have two ears.
What am I?

Answer: A horse.

Holly Harris (6)
St Peter's CE Primary School, Wrecclesham

Round And Round

It is a big, big, circle.
It has millions of animals.
It has lots of colours like a rainbow.
It has a lot of water.
It's in space.
It has big swirly mountains.
What am I?

Answer: *The world.*

Jessica Carys Ann Black (6)
St Peter's CE Primary School, Wrecclesham

Perfect Pet

When you are grumpy, I'll make you happy.
I bite really hard.
I am really cute.
I catch balls that have been thrown.
I eat bones.
I bark like this: *woof!*
What am I?

˙bop ∀ :ɹǝmsu∀

Haydn Woodhouse (7)
St Peter's CE Primary School, Wrecclesham

The Terrifying Team

My teeth are as sharp as a knife.
I live in the forest.
We don't get them in this country.
I always sneak up to my prey.
I am grey all around.
I live in a group.
What am I?

Answer: A wolf.

Lucas Pinto (7)
St Peter's CE Primary School, Wrecclesham

The Hopping Forest

I am as white as snow.
I like tapping my foot with a friend.
I like wiggling my ears.
I eat a lot of vegetables.
I have very tall ears.
I hop as high as a tree.
What am I?

Answer: A bunny.

Emilia Grace Collinson (6)
St Peter's CE Primary School, Wrecclesham

The Jungle Swinger

I have scary black eyes.
I have a tail as long as me.
I have brown arms and body.
I have stretchy arms.
I have giant feet.
I swing from tree to tree.
What am I?

Answer: A squirrel monkey.

Poppy Chua (7)
St Peter's CE Primary School, Wrecclesham

What Am I?

I have a long, swishy tail.
I have a black, wet nose.
I have an owner.
I have blue eyes.
I have paddled my feet in the filthy mud.
I stop when I want a drink.
What am I?

Answer: A dog.

Sophie Farrant (6)
St Peter's CE Primary School, Wrecclesham

Insect

I am as small as a stone.
I have black spots on my body.
I am as red as a post box.
I live on leaves.
I like to eat green leaves.
I use my wings to fly.
What am I?

Answer: A ladybird.

Kara Burch (6)
St Peter's CE Primary School, Wrecclesham

What Am I?

I like to lie down on the floor.
You can stroke me.
I pitter-patter around the garden.
When I'm settled, I like it when you stroke me.
I live in a house.
What am I?

Answer: A dog.

Amelie Kelley (6)
St Peter's CE Primary School, Wrecclesham

Roar

I am orange and black.
I have beady eyes.
I am as loud as a dragon.
I have sharp teeth and sharp claws.
I am as fierce as a lion.
I live in a jungle.
What am I?

Answer: A tiger.

Zane Harman (6)
St Peter's CE Primary School, Wrecclesham

My Magical Friend

I have four hooves like a horse.
I have a ponytail at the back of me.
I am as white as snow.
I have a horn like a goat.
I have a multicoloured mane.
What am I?

Answer: A unicorn.

Sharae Rattigan (6)
St Peter's CE Primary School, Wrecclesham

Leap

You can hear me.
You can touch me.
I move along.
I have round things on the bottom of me.
I go everywhere in the world.
I bump across the road.
What am I?

Answer: A bus.

Rylan Tucker (6)
St Peter's CE Primary School, Wrecclesham

Mysterious Master

I am fast on my feet.
I am mysterious.
I use weapons.
I am dangerous.
I am clever.
You will see me in China.
I wear black clothes.
What am I?

Answer: A ninja.

Victor Finn (7)
St Peter's CE Primary School, Wrecclesham

You Can Ride

I can run.
I can be big.
I come in brown, white and ginger.
I can live on a farm or I can be wild.
I can have friends.
I have hooves.
What am I?

Answer: A horse.

Chloe Scother (6)
St Peter's CE Primary School, Wrecclesham

The Woofy Superhero

I am brown as a dinosaur.
I run around every day.
I am so naughty.
I bark at cats.
I like bones to eat.
I always like to go on a walk.
What am I?

Answer: A dog.

Labeena Tahir (6)
St Peter's CE Primary School, Wrecclesham

What Am I?

I have long ears.
I have a fluffy tail.
I have some whiskers.
I hop on the grass.
I have four legs.
I like carrots to eat.
What am I?

Answer: A rabbit.

Jamie Potter (6)
St Peter's CE Primary School, Wrecclesham

Roar

I am as tall as a skyscraper.
I have sharp teeth.
I have sharp claws.
I eat meat.
I lived thousands of years ago.
What am I?

Answer: A dinosaur.

Patrick Doherty (6)
St Peter's CE Primary School, Wrecclesham

The Shadow

I use a sai, or shurikens or nunchucks
I wear dark colours.
My face is covered.
I am stealth.
I fight and protect.
What am I?

Answer: A ninja.

Dex Woods (7)
St Peter's CE Primary School, Wrecclesham

Tree Climber Of Australia

I have very fluffy ears.
People call me a bear.
I live in a gumtree where it's peaceful and quiet.
I like crawling and climbing up trees.
I hug trees at night while my mum hugs me tight.
I listen to the kookaburra laugh in the daytime.
I have time to hug my mum.
What am I?

Answer: A koala.

Matilda Harris (6)
The Dawnay School, Great Brookham

What Am I?

I am pretty and glittery.
I am silly and I am called Alice.
Cloppity and clickety go my hooves.
I climb mountains sometimes I live in a cave.
I love eating grass and leaves.
What am I?

Answer: A unicorn.

Paloma Rose Pardo (5)
The Dawnay School, Great Brookham

What Am I?

I am grey, black and white.
I have floppy ears.
I hop and hop all day long.
I live in a field and in a hole.
I like hopping in fields.
I like digging too.
What am I?

Answer: A rabbit.

Elly Edling-Hill (5)
The Dawnay School, Great Brookham

What Am I?

I look grey and white.
I would stroll along the floor.
I like to live outside and inside.
I like watching.
I don't like getting wet.
What am I?

Answer: A cat.

Sophie McIntosh (6)
The Dawnay School, Great Brookham

What Am I?

I am nice and I like the sun.
I like climbing trees.
I run along the trees.
I don't live in Africa.
I love the sun and the trees.
What am I?

Answer: A koala.

Eleanor Rourke (5)
The Dawnay School, Great Brookham

What Am I?

I look like a feathery yeti.
I live in a tree.
I fly.
I like eating rats.
I have a big yellow beak.
I have big wings.
What am I?

Answer: An eagle.

Joseph Osmond Gorman (5)
The Dawnay School, Great Brookham

What Am I?

I have a mane.
I have a big roar.
I am from Africa.
I have sharp claws.
I am from the cat family.
I eat meat.
What am I?

Answer: A lion.

Thomas Jenner (6)
The Dawnay School, Great Brookham

What Am I?

I am green.
I am colourful.
I move slowly as slow as a sloth.
I live in a ginormous tree.
I like camouflage.
What am I?

Answer: A chameleon.

Ruby Lane (5)
The Dawnay School, Great Brookham

What Am I?

I am orangish.
I fly.
I live in a castle.
I like blowing fire.
I have scaly skin
The knights ride on me.
What am I?

Answer: A dragon.

Riley Williams (6)
The Dawnay School, Great Brookham

What Am I?

I am white and cuddly.
I live in the Arctic.
I like to swim and catch fish.
I have big paws.
What am I?

Answer: A polar bear.

Francesca Louise Vlaeminck-Thomas (6)
The Dawnay School, Great Brookham

What Am I?

I look cute and small.
I move slowly.
I live in a house.
I like to play.
I like people.
What am I?

Answer: A puppy.

Lilly Ozturk (6)
The Dawnay School, Great Brookham

What Am I?

I am stripey.
I gallop.
I live in Africa.
I love eating.
I am black and white.
What am I?

Answer: A zebra.

Gloria Altersberger (5)
The Dawnay School, Great Brookham

What Am I?

I am grey and white.
I live in Africa.
I slither around.
I like biting people.
What am I?

Answer: A king cobra.

Luca Favero (6)
The Dawnay School, Great Brookham

What Am I?

I am stripy.
I gallop
I live in Africa.
I run along.
I am black and white.
What am I?

Answer: A zebra.

Georgina Hallett (5)
The Dawnay School, Great Brookham

What Am I?

I love to eat meat.
I love to get wet.
I love to eat people.
I am green.
What am I?

Answer: A crocodile.

Fred John Pilling (5)
The Dawnay School, Great Brookham

What Am I?

I am adventurous.
I love running.
I am stripy.
I live in Africa.
What am I?

Answer: A zebra.

Zac Lawrence (5)
The Dawnay School, Great Brookham

What Am I?

I am orange.
I move fast.
I love food.
What am I?

Answer: A tiger.

Freddie Stephens (5)
The Dawnay School, Great Brookham

Without This The World Is Horrid

It is warm and happy.
But does not have fur,
It is everlasting, but it can start at any time.
You cannot see it, but it can be everywhere.
This can break your heart, but it can mend it as well.
You can show it with a kiss or a hug.
What am I?

Answer: Love.

Evelyn Archer (7)
The Russell School, Richmond

Hot, Hot, Hot

I do not move, but I breathe fire.
I am filled with fire in my body.
I am not filled with coal.
I can be brown or grey.
I am bigger than the tallest person in the world.
I start to rumble before I breathe fire.
Who am I?

Answer: A volcano.

Josephine Elizabeth Bryant (6)
The Russell School, Richmond

At The Beach

I love you so much.
I love the wild waves that shimmer and glow.
I love the way the air is fresh.
The sand is wet between each toe.
The waves are as big as mountains.
The sun is bright and sets before night.
What is it?

Answer: The beach.

Sienna Scruby (6)
The Russell School, Richmond

What Am I?

I am a burning life-cycle.
I turn things from light green to dusty grey.
When I am gone, nature fights to restore.
The green people try to fight me,
But some life can't live without me.
What am I?

Answer: A forest fire.

Aurelia Kate Powell-Blyth (6)
The Russell School, Richmond

The Toy For A Boy

I love this toy.
This is the best for girl and boy.
I can build a house.
I can build a boat.
I will share the pieces with my friends.
We will play a lot.
What is it?

Answer: Lego.

Robert Raguzin (7)
The Russell School, Richmond

Ball

It has spikes.
It has a small tail.
It curls up into a ball.
It is bigger than an ant.
It is smaller than a bear.
It is as big as a rat.
What am I?

Answer: A hedgehog.

Henry Grimm (7)
The Russell School, Richmond

Colours

I am colourful.
I am a semi-circle.
You can see me up above the sky.
After the sun and rain.
I make people smile and happy.
What am I?

Answer: A rainbow.

Tasneem Sumaya Djerfi (7)
The Russell School, Richmond

"Witch" Animal Is It?

I am a pet.
I have a long tail.
I have whiskers.
I like to snooze.
I am as black as night.
I am a witch's pet.
What am I?

Answer: A black cat.

Sara Straffi (7)
The Russell School, Richmond

K-9

I come in different sizes.
I make lots and lots of friends.
I love going out for walks.
But mostly I like cuddles, when I'm not on guard.
My owners give me food to eat.
I can smell forty times better than humans.
I'm also known as man's best friend.
But have lots of different nicknames.
What am I?

Answer: A dog.

Amelia Fear (6)
Wood Street Infant School, Guildford

A Cold Day

I have a carrot nose.
You only see me when it snows.
I can't talk and I can't walk.
I melt in the sun.
When you build me it is fun.
What am I?

Answer: A snowman.

Jakub Miucci (5)
Wood Street Infant School, Guildford

Young Writers
Est.1991

YOUNG WRITERS INFORMATION

We hope you have enjoyed reading this book – and that you will continue to in the coming years.

If you're a young writer who enjoys reading and creative writing, or the parent of an enthusiastic poet or story writer, do visit our website **www.youngwriters.co.uk**. Here you will find free competitions, workshops and games, as well as recommended reads, a poetry glossary and our blog.

If you would like to order further copies of this book, or any of our other titles, then please give us a call or visit **www.youngwriters.co.uk**.

Young Writers
Remus House
Coltsfoot Drive
Peterborough
PE2 9BF
(01733) 890066
info@youngwriters.co.uk